The Battle Between Being "Mom" & "Boss"

HER THERAPY

Angel N. Livas

© **2019 Angel N. Livas**

All rights reserved. No parts of this book may be reproduced in any form whatsoever, by photography or xerography or by any other means, by broadcast or transmission, by translation into any kind of language, not by recording electronically or otherwise, without permission in writing from the author, except by a reviewer, who may quote brief passages in critical articles or reviews.

Published in Washington, DC by DC Media Connection. The author is represented by DC Media Connection 4928 Birch Lane, Alexandria, VA 22312 www.dcmediaconnection.com

ISBN-13: 978-1-7334652-0-5
Library of Congress Catalog Number: 2019912822
Printed in the United States of America
Cover Design: DC Media Connection
Layout Designer: Mahabub Alam

"For I know the plans I have for you," declares the LORD, "plans to prosper you and not to harm you, plans to give you hope and a future."
Jeremiah 29:11

TABLE OF CONTENTS

PREFACE 1

CHAPTER 1: THERE ARE NO ACCIDENTS 3

CHAPTER 2: WHO AM I? 15
   LETTERS TO MY SONS: A FAIR TRADE 25

CHAPTER 3: RELINQUISH THE GUILT 29
   LETTERS TO MY SONS: JUST ASK 37

CHAPTER 4: COMING TO GRIPS WITH FAILURE   **41**
   LETTERS TO MY SONS: I'M SORRY 59

CHAPTER 5: SACRIFICE V. COMPROMISE 61

CHAPTER 6: GETTIN' DOWN TO BUSINESS 67

CHAPTER 7: THE PROVERBS WOMAN 85
   LETTERS TO MY SONS: VISION 2020: THE RESET 89

RESOURCES **93**

THANK YOU **99**

ABOUT THE AUTHOR **101**

PREFACE

"She speaks with wisdom, and faithful instruction is on her tongue."
~Proverbs 31:26

Days seem long and nights seem short. If your life looks anything like mine - your once demanding work schedule has been replaced by your new role as your kids "home-school teacher". Your nights are a-tug-of-war between productivity and your pillow...and somehow you're managing to keep it all together amid the global pandemic that is COVID-19.

Your world will never be the same. Not because you're in quarantine - but, because you now have an opportunity to reintroduce yourself to your household. You always felt engaged in your child's life... just maybe not active. It wasn't for a lack of interest - but, you couldn't figure out how to win the battle between motherhood and conquering your business goals.

>> HER THERAPY

For many of us we spent the majority of our lives working towards acquiring a certain status within our industries. It wasn't that we didn't want to have kids (for some of us) - it was just not our top priority. As we gaze at the miniature versions of ourselves, today, guilt slowly creeps into our psyche and makes us feel bad for who we once dreamed of being.

Whether you find yourself living out your dream or feel trapped because you have lost your way...I pray that this book serves as an agent of change to show you that it is possible to walk boldly in your purpose - - without the guilt. If you find that this book empowers you to hold your head up a little higher and replaces the pep you once had in your step - I'll feel as though I did my job.

I encourage you to embark upon this journey with me, and when the last page has turned you'll have an opportunity to connect with our therapeutic community. But, for now I want you to relax and prepare to receive practical skills and tangible take-aways that will help you alleviate the imposter thoughts (that you can't successfully manage your role as mom and boss)... because this book is a testament that you can.

{2}

CHAPTER 1
THERE ARE NO ACCIDENTS

"Her children arise up, and call her blessed"
~Proverbs 31:28

It felt like slow motion. I braced for impact. Clutching the armrest and the door handle. My legs locked under the glove compartment. Then it happened. The car slammed into the guardrail. Flying into the air... completing six somersaults before landing on the driver's side.

Completely shaken, I proceeded to climb through the passenger window, until I heard a moan from the driver.

What do I do? Save myself... or try to pull him out too?

I opted for the latter until we realized that he couldn't move. As he screamed in pain and fear - I pulled myself through the shattered passenger window, only to see a body outlined in blood in the snow nearly 10-feet from the car. In that moment I began to understand the severity of the accident. The pouring rain continued to wash the blood from the motionless body that had once occupied the backseat.

I began to pace back and forth to keep my muscles active and engaged... instead of people driving by, they pulled over to show their concern. One lady was in tears, saying that she had witnessed the entire accident... and prayed that the passengers survived. Others stopped and dropped off sweatshirts, blankets or merely stayed with us until the police and ambulances arrived. These strangers became my Angels. They showed me compassion and love on that cold January day... and nearly fifteen years later - I can mark that encounter as the day that changed my life.

It was approximately 3 weeks before my 21st birthday. A friend and I were headed to grab breakfast - when his cousin decided he wanted to tag along. My friend asked if he could drive my car... and against my better judgement I said, "Sure". It wasn't long after we hit 295-S in Washington, DC - that I found myself saying, "Please slow down". Shortly after those words left my mouth, the car hydroplaned across 2-lanes of traffic before we struck the front-end of the interstate's guardrail.

The impact from the accident caused the driver's lung to collapse and left both him and the backseat passenger in intensive care. As for me... I walked away with a small scar on my right shin. Aside for the overall recovery of my co-passengers, my gravest concern was how I was going to explain the accident to my parents.

Back at Howard University Hospital, on the very campus I was sent to pursue my undergraduate studies, I can recall the doctor sitting with me in my assigned patient room asking me a series of questions to determine how I was feeling. He then explained the level of disbelief that he and the other doctors and nurses had when they realized I had been in the same car as the two gentlemen who were brought in on stretchers and sent to intensive care. I was told that I was very fortunate and blessed to have walked out of that car. He even took his comments one step further and said, "God must have a mighty assignment for you."

In that moment, I didn't have an epiphany... nor did I really *hear* what the doctor was telling me. It wasn't until I crashed into "adult problems," nearly a decade later, that his words resurfaced. It's funny how traumatic memories embed themselves in one's subconscious... only to be retrieved, unbidden, at a later date.

Through moments of reflection I've learned many things from that accident but, the greatest lesson it taught me was that I could have died at the tender age of 20. Yet... I survived... for a reason.

Remember those "adult problems" I mentioned? Well, let's just say (FIVE) miscarriages have a way of making you feel like you've failed at motherhood... and being a woman.

I was 28 the first time it happened. While celebrating the recent exchange of our weddings vows, I can recall a gentle whisper telling me not to partake in libations during our southern Caribbean honeymoon. When I first heard the voice I totally ignored it, I mean the waitress had literally just brought me a pomegranate margarita.

However, the replay of those words "you're pregnant" didn't subside until I returned home and I confirmed my suspicions. My excitement about becoming a mother completely overpowered all of the bad choices I had made after hearing the quiet whispers. I completely ignored the drinking, the jet skiing, the horseback riding, the zip-lining and all of the other adventurous activities I chose to partake in throughout the course of that week.

As I prepared for my first obstetrician appointment, I had nervous energy, anxious thoughts, and a level of excitement that I can't even begin to express.

Nothing could have ruined that day...or so, I thought.

The nurse was very nice, as I remember her telling me, "Maybe you're not as far along as you thought". In my spirit, I immediately knew something was wrong...but, I was hopeful that everything would work out in the end. I laid stretched out on the cold hard table waiting for the radiologist to confirm the gestation of my pregnancy. Never did I imagine that my energy would soon mirror that of the surface holding me up.

The doctor grabbed the doppler and I could feel its cold sensation glide across my belly...he pushed, stroked up and down and finally said there is no heartbeat. Though he quickly added that I might not be as far along as I'd thought...a tear slowly seeped from my eyes.

When I returned to the office two weeks later the sac was deformed and they told me that I had a "missed-miscarriage" or a silent or delayed miscarriage. According to the miscarriage association, a missed miscarriage is defined as the baby has died or failed to develop, but your body has not actually expelled him or her.

Because there had been no evidence of fetal development for several weeks, the doctor prescribed me medication to speed up the miscarriage process. They advised me to take the day off, as I could possibly experience cramping, bleeding, etc. So, I adhered to the doctor's requests and spent the day at home. After orally consuming the small circular pills and waiting for something to magically happen, I was surprised when nothing did. I called the nurse and they ended up calling in a different prescription - but, advised that I insert these pills vaginally. I can recall asking the nurse if she was sure I should do such a thing. She chuckled and said, "Yes, it's safe. It will just speed up the process".

To my horror, a few minutes after having the pills inserted - I broke out in hives. The palms of my hands turned bright red and itchy, my insides felt like they were playing a game of peek-a-boo. I could not understand what was happening. Shortly after realizing I was having an allergic reaction to the medicine, my husband drove me to the emergency room. I literally felt like I was in full term labor. After hours of contractions, cramps, peek-a-boo pains... what ever you'd like to call it... they ended up prepping me for an emergency surgery.

The first miscarriage was by far the worst, physically - but, all five took something away from me that can never be replenished.

After the third miscarriage I was sent to Shady Grove Fertility Clinic in Annandale, Virginia where they ran every test under the sun on me. I can recall asking if they were going to also test my husband, because I was the only person being poked and probed at the time. They told me that they only needed him to bring in a semen sample for them to examine. With attitude and fiery I asked "is that all he has to do?" and they quickly said, "Yes."

Meanwhile, I was being injected with Iodine, flipped upside down on machines, and undergoing all types of other testing to figure out what was going wrong. The doctors didn't seem to have any solid leads. They just said that, during the chromosomal structuring, the baby was either receiving too many of one chromosome or not enough of others.

According to the American Pregnancy Association, a mere 1% of couples experience 3 or more consecutive first trimester miscarriages, or recurrent miscarriages. And I just so happened to be a part of that 1%.

After the fourth miscarriage, the doctor told me that due to my recurrent miscarriages, my chances of successfully having a baby without scientific interference was less than 25%.

I'll be honest - I don't remember anything else after those words. All I heard was that the one thing I believed my body was created to do... it was not allowing me to. I was failing for the first time in my life.

Throughout that 2 year period, I didn't feel like there was anyone who would understand my situation, not even my husband. I prayed a lot and relied on faith. I truly believed that a logical explanation would soon reveal itself.

Fast forward about a year from my fifth miscarriage, and I was blessed beyond measure. Without explanation or scientific influence, I delivered a beautiful baby boy, about six weeks shy of my 30th birthday.

Some people might look at me as being stubborn and bull headed - because I didn't care what the doctors told me. But, in my mind and in my heart, I didn't believe it was their place to tell me what I was incapable of, when I know the Source of my possibilities.

So, instead of paying upwards of $10,000 for treatments - I tithed a little more, prayed a little harder and remained faithful in my requests. In the end, I believe that God delivered me the desires of my heart. And just as Noah carried civilization through the floods for 40-days and nights... my first born child, Noah, was the rainbow on the other side of my 2-year storm.

The car accident and my fertility challenges are two of the most trying situations that have directly impacted who I am. I am sharing these difficult periods of my life because it is necessary in understanding Angel, the Boss and the Mom.

It's imperative that we establish a sense of trust and understanding before we embark upon this journey. We have all faced moments of fear, feeling inadequate, and rejection. It's my hope that, by being vulnerable and unapologetically honest about my truth, that you too will find your voice and truth.

Now, don't leave me alone on this journey... join me and together we'll find healing and a mutually sound surface to stand on as Mom and Boss.

{12}

The Battle

What obstacles have you had to overcome that might impact how you parent and/or do business?

Can you identify at least two incidents that might have appeared as accidents - but, you later realized were blessings?

Have you experienced a traumatic encounter that you have not honestly dealt with, yet?

The Solution

Take some time to think back as far as you can to identify emotions that you might have felt from your childhood. We're not in search of one type of emotion - so, document the things that made you happy, sad, afraid, excited, etc.

If you have experienced any type of trauma in your life - I challenge you to speak to a trusted neutral source to aid you in completely overcoming the experience. I personally believe in (and love) therapy, but I understand that everyone doesn't feel that way.

CHAPTER 2
WHO AM I?

*"She is clothed with strength and dignity;
she can laugh at the days to come."*

~Proverbs 31:25

Mom, Daughter, Sister, Friend... are the most important titles that I hold... but, right up there with those, you'll find Founder & CEO. To my boys, I'm "Mom". But, to thousands of others, I'm the Founder of "The Woman Behind The Business," a nonprofit that assists women entrepreneurs, c-suite executives, and political figures in building national and international business relationships to expand their brand, network, and net worth.

>> HER THERAPY

I wouldn't say that roles or positions truly define who I am... or anybody, for that matter. But, for some reason - most people use these as identifiers when asked, "Who are you?".

As a kid, I loved being the class advocate. I would stand up for the quiet kid others would peg as targets for harassment and teasing. In most instances, I would be in the background encouraging them to stand up for themselves; and in others I'd intervene with a swift response to shock and shut up the aggressor. I guess you could say I've always been passionate about people being treated with dignity and respect.

To that end, I was never afraid to use my voice to encourage the soft-spoken (to standup for him/herself)... or speak on behalf of the individual who was too afraid to speak at all. So, as you can imagine - my mouth has gotten me into trouble (at times), but it has also created a lot of opportunities for me.

Having a well-rounded understanding of who you are is essential to you "owning" your purpose. So now, I want us to go on a journey together. But, in order for us to truly reach a moment of truth, we have to take a few moments to reflect.

{16}

Why are you reflecting?, you might ask. Reflection is a powerful tool! It literally allows you to put time and space between your thoughts, decisions and actions, to provide a well-rounded perspective on situations. Being able to reflect back to our childhood will allow us to examine the core of who we are.

For the next 2-3 minutes I want you to think about things that you loved doing as a child. It's great to consider things you enjoyed - but, I want you to delve deep... think about those things that your family might reminiscence on, or the things you constantly hear them say... like, "oh, she's been doing that her entire life"!

I must have been about seven or eight years-old when I put on my first "after church" play for my parents. Now, I have no idea how I came up with the concept, but, the implementation came naturally to me. After church there wasn't much on basic television besides M.A.S.H. and Star Trek and ... let's just say I wasn't a fan of either. So, I hyped up my big brother and little sister to be a part of my improv skits. At the time, I had no idea what "improv" meant... but, there I was creating themes and challenging my siblings to act them out!

{17}

>> HER THERAPY

The real creativity came into play when I started designing program books, tickets, and invitations to accompany the Sunday evening performances.

It wasn't until earlier this year that I took a moment to reflect on those early childhood memories, and truly identified and embraced my innate gifts. You know... those tendencies you have or natural abilities that no one had to teach you...yup! Those would be your innate gifts.

Well, during that afternoon of reflection I realized that my oldest son is almost at the same age that I was when I first started displaying my natural talents.

So, of course it caused me to be more attentive to his behaviors. I want to be able to cultivate his natural talents, while exposing him to as many experiences, cultures, and industries as I possibly can.

So, how can a busy mom that's managing both a household and a business have her radar open to monitor those special qualities of her child(ren). It's not as hard as you might think... but, it will require you to pay attention. And when you find it...

you might be surprised by how your talents and your child's might just make for a fun "joint-venture".

My oldest had to be just over four-years old when he started running to the kitchen to help me prepare dinner, after school. At first, I just thought he enjoyed spending time in the kitchen with Mommy (smile)... but, after a while, I learned that he was really interested in the cooking process. This, naturally, drew the youngest (who was two years old) into the kitchen. However, I quickly learned that he was more interested in eating the food - than cooking. But, what I recognized was that we were creating memories. The experience drew us closer together, it was fun, they were learning, and they were 100% engaged in the process.

During that time, 2016, the "Black Lives Matter" movement had become very prominent, as a number of young African-American boys were being shot and killed by police officers throughout the United States.

As a journalist, the negative news that was constantly invading our homes, news feeds, and newspapers attracted me to the idea of creating a positive television program with an all African-American male cast.

So, I asked my boys if they would be interested in creating a cooking show. They said, "Yes".

I reached out to one of my friends who happens to be a celebrity chef... he was in! Then, I asked my line sister if her son would be interested in being a part of the cast. And just like that "Kiddie Kitchen" was born. It's now two years later, and the show is still airing on local television and on a few online platforms.

It has truly been an amazing journey because - it's created a space for me to teach the boys about public speaking, business, finance, their appearance, and of course cooking.

You see, I took a skill that I have in creating content and married that with an interest that my children have. Now, story-telling is at the core of who I am. I enjoy helping people and companies tell their story, while also connecting them to their target audience. However, in this case, I was able to establish an even deeper connection with my boys.

Developing this show also allowed my children to see Mommy at work. It helped them to grasp what mommy does when I'm not at home... while also allowing my natural gifts to further propel theirs.

{20}

I'm a firm believer that in order for the two worlds to co-exist, peacefully, you must introduce your children to your work. If they can grasp, "Oh this is what Mommy is doing when she's not with me", or... "This is where Mommy is when she's not at home."... then they can adjust to your absence.

For instance, my boys have attended a number of my speaking engagements over the past 2 years. So, now if I tell them Mommy has to travel for work, my youngest, Nelson, will ask, "Mommy, are you going to talk to people"? And I can confidently say, "Yes," because I know he has his own interpretation of what that means.

Don't allow yourself to get lost in a role. You can claim your title as "Mom" AND, "Boss" but, at the heart of it lies your ability to be a leader.

THE BATTLE

Introducing your children to a well-rounded you. Do you successfully share your gifts and talents with your kids?

Have you evaluated your child(ren's) talents?

Do you struggle to find creative ways for you and your children to spend time together (that doesn't include being on a device or watching television)?

The Solution

Try exposing your children to various facets of who you are. Take them to work with you. Allow them to attend business events (when appropriate).

If you've identified your children's innate gifts, consider finding a fun way to marry their likes with your strengths. You might be surprised by what you discover.

LETTERS TO MY SONS

A Fair Trade

Leaving never gets easier, although as you grow older, I know you'll understand what it means when Mommy says, "Ok, boys, Mommy has to go out of town for work..."

This week I traveled to Miami, FL to attend the NATPE Miami Marketplace Conference 2019. The underlying goal was to

>> HER THERAPY

pitch two television concepts to distributors for national and international airing. The response was overwhelming – so many people loved the idea of 3 young boys, all under the age of 6, cooking in the kitchen with a celebrity chef.

Our concept was extremely well-received and we even walked away with a few contract offers.

With every day, a new blessing awaits you!

Today, I was provided the opportunity to meet "The Woman Behind" Muhammad Ali's famous poems ... Khalilah Camacho Ali, his first wife. This moment changed my life. Not because I met this absolutely unapologerically honest woman but, her story was beautiful ... pure and untold. Then, as fate would have it, she introduced me to her manager... and he introduced me to the owner of Avant Protege, a talent management company based right in my backyard. It's amazing how sometimes

{26}

God pulls us out of our comfort zones (or immediate community) to connect us to the very person who can change our lives.

Now, I haven't shared my journey to entrepreneurship too many times, but today I shared it with Ms. Ali. I traded vulnerability for freedom... and owned my truth.

It was in that moment that she said, "We want to help you...". Whatever "help" looks like, that conversation energized me. It is another opportunity I've been afforded to expand my brand and network.

Mommy will be back home by morning.

~ Love, Mom

>> HER THERAPY

CHAPTER 3
Relinquish The Guilt

*"She sees that her trading is profitable,
and her lamp does not go out at night."*
~Proverbs 31:18

Why do I feel like the absolute worst mother on earth when I leave the children behind to pursue other ambitions?

Last year, I was asked over a dozen times by women in Africa, Canada, the Caribbean, and the United States, "How do you leave your children and not feel guilty?"

The first time I was asked... I hadn't even equated the emotion I was feeling to guilt. I just knew I was frantically juggling the two most important things in my life... pursuing my purpose and being a great mom.

It wasn't until I sat on a stage in Accra, Ghana and a new mom asked me, "How do you combat the Mommy Guilt?" that I realized that many women with children are fighting off guilt.

Prior to launching my media firm I worked for AARP, the largest membership organization in the United States. My boss was Myrna Blyth a legendary media mogul who was a part of launching major magazines during her heyday.

I remember walking into her office, while I was maybe 8-months pregnant with my second son. She asked me if I was planning to return to work... or if I desired to be a stay-at-home mom. I can recall looking at her like she was crazy to even consider me to be the stay-at-home mom type. She quickly read my face, and said, "Ok good, because your boys will respect you so much for returning to work".

At the time, I wasn't quite sure why she thought my kids would value me more for having my own career but, today I understand. Well, at least I have my own interpretation of why it's important to establish your own identity.

When my siblings and I were growing up, my mom stayed at home with us and could essentially cater to her children. This was very important to my mom.

But, as we grew older, Mom explored entrepreneurship. I can honestly say that I have more memories of me and my siblings working in the family business than I do of just being home with our mom after school.

I learned many valuable lessons, but having two entrepreneurial parents in my household taught me what being a business owner was all about.

"What they see is what they'll be" is the motto for the international organization 100 Black Men of America, Inc. I love this organization because of their commitment to the intellectual development of youth and the economic empowerment of African American communities.

When we expose our children to life outside of a 9-to-5 they know that something more exists. They are no longer held in the mental bondage that going to school and getting a job are the only roads to the American Dream. With their horizons broadened, their possibilities feel more like opportunities...

opposed to the confines that are often the end goals taught in our educational systems.

So, why do we feel guilty if we're actually providing a positive perspective for our children? I think for some of us this answer will vary. However, for many of us it's a blend between adhering to societal standards and ensuring that our child(ren) never feel as though we're choosing work over them.

Let's be brutally honest for a moment. How many times have you felt guilty because you've observed how your girlfriend tends to her children or spends more time developing various skills within her child(ren)? Meanwhile you're beating yourself up because you struggle to provide home cooked meals and assistance with homework. Trust me I know.

But, instead of holding onto the notion that "She's a better mom than I am." (In this specific case it's my line sister.) I tell Ashley all the time how much I love her engagement with her kids and how much I wish I had all of her amazing "teacher" qualities (i.e. patience).

But, you know what happens when I'm willing to be vulnerable... she reciprocates. That's when I learn that she equally examines and borrows methods from my interactions with my boys.

Do you know how liberating those unapologetically honest conversations are? Don't hold on to the nasty, yucky things that leave you feeling bad and questioning your allegiance to your children. Address the emotions... and release them.

You know the Rhianna song with the hook that says "Work, work, work, work, work"... that is me. If I could brainstorm business ideas with individuals or help craft their stories around the clock, I most likely would. My work energizes me. It is fulfilling and... at the end of every day... I can typically see the fruits of my labor through the successes of others.

Now, think back to Chapter 1 - "There are No Accidents." Remember how I fought for my sons? That's what keeps them number one...even with the work. It's funny how moments that are so hard to deal with when you're in the midst, are the very things that help you appreciate your blessings all the more.

Had I not endured those difficult years of losing fetus after fetus, I've sometimes wondered how committed I would have been to keeping my children my number one priority.

{33}

>> HER THERAPY

Today, I can say without reservation that my boys are my "Why". I want them to be just as much a part of the business as I am.

Currently, they're the one's on camera... but, eventually, they'll be the one's flying the drones and storyboarding our shoots if they so desire.

See, I combat the negative thoughts of my children possibly feeling second to my work by ensuring that I focus on Quality versus Quantity, which we'll delve into deeper in Chapter 4.

But, the overall concept is to make sure that the time allocated for interacting with your children is Quality Time.

{34}

The Battle

What are the underlying reasons for your guilt?

Do you allow what other people think about your time spent with your children to impact you (positively or negatively?) Or the decisions you make?

The Solution

Imagine that your child is all grown up and headed to college. Based on your current parenting methods, have you created a life that revolves completely around your child(ren)?

If so, is that what you ultimately want?

Think about the life that you ultimately want for you and your family. It shouldn't be one-sided... all about the child(ren)... or all about you. Finding balance can sometimes feel like a cat chasing its tail. But, with proper strategy it is possible.

LETTERS TO MY SONS

JUST ASK

It was totally unexpected. I was on a shoot for a college friend when I overheard another alumni of Howard University talking about a program that she works on as part of her role as a diplomat in the United States government. The "Start Up Entrepreneurship" program sounded like something that could be of significant benefit to the nonprofit that I founded... "The Woman Behind The Business" (WBB).

>> HER THERAPY

So, I asked a few questions about the program and was informed that the application process would close at the end of the day. However, she told me that, if I wanted to apply, she would send me more information.

So, during the shoot – I took the time to complete the application – but, was hesitant to send it off – since I wasn't sure, specifically, how a nonprofit would benefit.

She gave me a slight nudge to just submit it. And so, before I left... I did. A few days later I was informed that some of the program's representatives wanted to speak with me further. Ultimately, I was invited to participate in the Caribbean Road to GES 2019, which was slated to take place in Curaçao, Netherlands.

So, here is where the dilemma happened.... I had already purchased tickets for us (my boys and myself) to spend the latter part of

{38}

the week in Orlando for my niece, Kairi's birthday! There was no way I could cancel the Disney trip... but I didn't want to miss the opportunity to expand WBB's international presence.

So, I went back to the facilitators of the Start Up to find out if I could participate solely in the start-up portion of the program... forfeiting my slot to pitch at the Caribbean GES 2019.

To my surprise it all worked out... but, I would have never known that the option was available had I not asked.

So, I left the Netherlands early Thursday morning ... with just enough time to grab you boys and hop on another flight that evening to Orlando.

Was I tired?... Absolutely. Did it kill me? No.

>> HER THERAPY

To me, this provided me an opportunity to take a few steps back to organize a few essential elements for my nonprofit. Then, I aligned my schedule to ensure that I could have uninterrupted time with my boys... and my family.

I wasn't worried about answering emails, or fulfilling client requests during our time together in Florida... you all had my undivided attention. And most importantly to me... I fulfilled my promise to you!

~ Love Mom

CHAPTER 4
Coming
To Grips With Failure

> *"She sets about her work vigorously;*
> *her arms are strong for her tasks."*
> ~Proverbs 31:17

Failure. It's a hard pill to swallow…when you realize that your world is crumbling down because of your actions or lack there of. How do you cope?

I know that people tell us not to look at those moments as failures. We are encouraged to view those occurrences as "lessons learned". But, what happens when those very lessons cause you to second-guess who you are?

>> HER THERAPY

It's always been easier for me to cope with putting out office fires than emotional ones. I do my best not to fall short with anything that I do... I mean, I'm an extreme overachiever. So, when I mess up on any level, I take it hard.

When I first started my company, DC Media Connection, I had the opportunity to work with a local nonprofit that was celebrating their 20th year in service. They were planning a huge gala with live performances, an awards presentation and all the bells and whistles to make for a spectacular evening.

When I was approached with the idea... I knew my team and I could pull it off. The problem was... I was a team of one. I knew plenty of business owners to collaborate with... but, wasn't sure how the client would "take" to any of the companies that I brought to the table. You see, the client was an older woman and... let's just say... she was extremely meticulous.

Now, my first mistake was making myself available to this client around the clock. She would call and email all hours of the night with questions and concerns.

{42}

At first, I graciously responded immediately...setting a horrible precedent. Honestly, I was just excited to have my first six-figure contract, so, I was eager to go above and beyond.

Then, because of the expectations that I'd set - she started expecting the same level of availability from all of the team members that I'd brought onboard.

As you know, most companies don't operate how I'd led her to believe.

And that's when things went from bad to worse.

She ended up firing the event planning company the same month the event was slated to take place. She hated all of their ideas, yet she wanted them to have innovative concepts readily available to dissect daily. This created a very hostile environment and... as the person responsible for managing it all... I was miserable.

It was the first project that I was very intentional about subcontracting work to other dynamic small businesses. However, some people get so comfortable with working with you (or your company) that they almost never give anyone else a chance.

>> HER THERAPY

Now, I managed to connect this client with one of my event planning clients at the last minute -and... while there were still complaints... we managed to pull off a sold out event with over 150 attendees.

So, you're probably wondering where "failure" came into play. Well, when the event was over the client told us to take the Monday off in celebration of the successful event.

I was so happy the event was over I turned in the last invoice to be paid and I was ready to close out that contract. I ended up getting a call from her inquiring if I interviewed any of the attendees or captured any quotes to be compiled in the post event press release.

I can remember sitting on the phone feeling like I'd failed this woman tremendously. As the emcee for the event I hadn't planned to capture interviews.

But, when she found out I had not done the post event interviews or press release, she fired me.

Granted the event I was hired to produce was executed flawlessly (except for the post event wrap-up) so, I didn't take it personally. If anything, I was relieved and excited to finally be

{44}

done with that contract. I felt like a weight had been lifted from my shoulders. From time to time, I think about how much I learned from that experience and how it taught me about the types of clients I am willing to work with.

Emotionally, I think I leave much to be desired. I don't like situations that involve excess drama... and I definitely don't care for conversations that require me to tap into my emotional side.

This is interesting, because I require my children to share how they're feeling and I always try to make sure that I am transparent about how *their* behaviors make *me* feel.

So, one weekend we were driving home after my oldest son's last football game of the season, and he had been awarded a sportsmanship medal.

As I was driving, I looked in the rearview mirror and told him I was very proud of him (especially since he had scored the team's only touchdown right before the buzzer). He was very gracious. He smiled and said thank you. Then, I heard a softer voice...my younger son... who said, "Are you proud of me too?"

I immediately, said, "Of course". Then, he hit me with a question I wasn't prepared for-

{45}

>> HER THERAPY

"Well, why didn't you come to my T-ball game when I got my trophy? I missed you."

My heart sank.

I didn't try to sugar-coat the situation. I had to be honest and tell him that I missed him too... and that, unfortunately, mommy hadn't realized that it was the last game of the season.

The worse part about the situation is that I wasn't doing anything. I honestly had thought the game had been cancelled (because it had rained earlier in the day) so, I was just doing extra work at the office.

Now, I wish that his dad had sent a message to say - "Hey, the game is on." But... at the end of the day... it wasn't his responsibility. So, I owed my son a heart-felt apology. After I expressed how sorry I was for missing his special day, he said, "It's ok, Mommy, I knew you wanted to be there... can I have some ice cream?" And I knew all was right in his world (as long as he got his ice cream).

Creating a safe space for your children to express themselves is so important. While I hated the circumstances (having to acknowledge my shortcomings), being the "beta" that allowed

{46}

my children to feel open to share their emotions with me... made me grateful for the outcome.

From that experience and others - I developed the Q.U.I.E.T method.

- » **Quality/Quantity**
- » **Understanding**
- » **Intentional**
- » **Expression**
- » **Transparency**

Sometimes when we are "shamed", we're quick to try to talk ourselves out of the situation or circumstance. Instead I encourage you to try the Q.U.I.E.T method.

Quality / Quantity

First, examine yourself to determine if you have been putting in Quality Time. You might be with your children a lot... but, if you're not actually spending time interacting and engaging with them, your "q's" are off balance.

What I've found to be true is children remember the Quality Time that you spend with them, even if it's not often.

{47}

>> HER THERAPY

And honestly, this is true in business as well. You can show up to work every day... but, if you haven't produced anything of quality during your time in the office... your presence is not fruitful.

That's why I have created routines with my children, to ensure that we have our special, personal experiences throughout the week.

For instance, during our drive to school we recite our daily affirmations. This is something I started with my boys shortly after my oldest turned 3-years old and the idea came to me after seeing the movie The Help. In the movie the maid would ask the little girl that she cared for to recite the following words, *"You is kind. You is smart. You is important."*

While her sentence structure might have been grammatically incorrect, it was the concept that inspired me to pour positivity over my kids daily.

So, I developed my own set of affirmations, by using the first 5-letters of the alphabet:

"I am **A**mazing. I am **B**rilliant. I am **C**onfident. I am **D**etermined. and I am **E**xcellent!" ... and on **E**xcellent, they throw their hands in the air with excitement!

{48}

Another ritual that I started with my boys about a year ago was establishing a bedtime routine. Instead of merely kissing them goodnight - I sing "Yes, Jesus Loves Me"... and they join in at certain parts of the song.

Then my youngest says a prayer (which can sometimes be one of those long drawn out prayers), followed by my oldest's prayer... and I close it out with my prayer, kisses and hugs.

So... even though I might not be with my boys all of the time... I believe that it is because of these rituals that our bond is so strong. Just remember... Quality Time is what's most important.

Understanding

When an issue is being presented to you, be present... and quiet. Do not sit thinking of your rebuttal. Honestly, be still... and be attentive to the conversation at hand.

I don't think it's ever your children's intention to outright degrade you or make you feel bad...but, your response will determine how they address similar situations in the future.

>> HER THERAPY

It's essential to your relationship that you listen with an understanding ear and open heart.

For instance my son was having a hard time in school immediately following my divorce. I remember asking him about a particular incident and he wasn't being truthful (and we both knew it). I quickly squatted to be at eye level with him, and I explained that if he couldn't be honest with me - I couldn't protect or defend him. I then went biblical (they attend a Christian School) and asked what does the Bible say? He lowered his head and mumbled "honor my mother and father" ... I in turn said - are you honoring me right now? He began to weep and eventually told me the truth. To this day, I can literally see his mind calculating the risk that goes along with being honest or not...and so far he's chosen to do the right thing. However, if every time he told the truth I flipped out - it would make his calculations a lot harder. So, I don't. I remember what it was like to be a kid ... and if I want to build a solid, honest and open communication line with my children... I can't flip out. Their punishments have to align with the behavior choices.

I always make it a point to explain that I appreciate their honesty and why they're being reprimanded.

Intentional

How much emphasis do you place on the one thing in life that you're given every day... for free. Yet, if you don't use it, you lose it.

I some times do this exercise where I ask my audience, "If I were to give you $86,400 dollars every day, how would you spend it?" The only caveats are - you can't save any of it... and what you don't use you lose.

For about 10-minutes people can come up with all types of ways to not waste the money. Yet... when I flip the variable from being money to the amount of seconds they are given every day... the room grows silent. People realize how much time they waste...and unfortunately, they're more excited and more engaged with the idea of spending $86,400 a day, versus being intentional with how their Time is spent.

I say all of this to say that Time matters. In business we say that "Time is money". But... when it comes to how we manage our Time with our families... there is less emphasis on its value.

Be Intentional. Think about this for a moment. When you receive a call confirming a meeting that you've been waiting to

>> HER THERAPY

have … you don't just leave it to chance that you'll remember the date and time…you take the time to schedule it on your calendar. Actually, it doesn't even have to be a big meeting…it's anything that's of importance to you - you schedule it into your life (hair appointments, a night out with friends, spa appointments, etc). So, why not be just as intentional with scheduling time with your kids?

Plan outings for you and your family. I personally believe in spending quality time with my boys together and individually. When you make your children a priority, opposed to an option they can feel the difference. I know my boys appreciate when I put my phone down, or close my laptop and give them my undivided attention. It's not hard … you just have to be willing to evaluate the situation and decide what's more important in that moment.

I challenge you to always be accountable for your family time. Take the Time to schedule all of your children's important events. Make Time to volunteer at your child's school. Set aside Time to go on at least one field trip with your child throughout the school year.

{52}

And if you should ever run into one of those uncomfortable situations when your child expresses something that you've done that hurt their feelings... set a deadline for yourself to respond in a timely manner. Don't allow negative energy to fester in your home. Address it. Apologize, if necessary. And keep your family dynamics... dynamic.

Expression

Creating an environment for your children to be able to openly express how they're feeling is key to maintaining a happy and healthy relationship.

Think about your relationship with your parents or the relationship between your friends and their parents. Did you ever wish that you had a more "honest" relationship with your parents as a child? Do you have a hard time expressing how you feel, because you are accustomed to suppressing your own feelings? If so, here is your chance to break that cycle.

If you had parents who allowed you to be vocal about what you liked and didn't, then you might not have to work so much in this area. But, for anyone who grew up feeling like your voice was silenced - this is especially important for you to provide your child a little more freedom of expression.

If you travel a lot or trust your children to be under the care of others, it's so very important to maintain clear lines of communication. If your child doesn't communicate with you, or... worse... feel as though they don't have to communicate with you because "You're never around, anyway" - you have to be more Intentional and Understanding during your interactions with your child.

Transparency

Would you consider yourself to be fairly open with your children? Do your children get to see a well-rounded perspective of who you really are? I believe that being transparent with your children helps to build their emotional intelligence.

My recommendations are solely based on my personal experiences. There's no scientific evidence that I've gathered to prove this...however, I stand behind my recommendation whole heartedly.

To be quite frank, I often find myself wanting to shelter my children from bad, sad or adverse situations. I think we all do. However, I've learned that we have to take strides towards being open, honest, transparent and even vulnerable at times to help build their confidence when dealing with their own emotions.

When COVID-19 took the life of my first cousin - I was devastated and sad that I couldn't be near my family. However, I felt this need to put on my super-mom cape and continue to function as my children's home-school teacher, since I didn't want them to fall behind with their classwork. By the end of the day...I couldn't control my emotions any longer. I found myself hurrying to wipe away my tears as I heard little feet pedaling towards me. During their nighttime ritual we talked about my cousin and they prayed for our family. I'm not certain why I didn't want to share the news with them - but, I was pleasantly surprised by their level of interest and concern. The next morning they asked to see pictures of our cousin and inquired about her having children.

It became a teachable moment for all of us. I learned that children are a lot more resilient and understanding than we often give them credit. I believe that I was afraid to be emotionally

>> HER THERAPY

transparent with my children because it's the one area of my being that I rarely tap in to. However, I recognized the tremendous disservice I was providing them ... none of us should ever have to hide our true emotions. Especially not in the safe quarters of one's home. So, I challenge you to create an emotionally safe and secure haven for your family. A space that allows you and the children to feel free to express your true emotions.

The Battle

How do you balance your kids' schedules with your own?

Have you missed an important event for your child(ren)? How did it make you feel?

Have you found yourself blaming others for your inability to always be available to your child(ren)?

How can you see yourself implementing the Q.U.I.E.T. method?

The Solution

Create a family calendar or add your children's activities/events to your work calendar. You can even color code your family activities (on your work calendar) to ensure they pop out at you daily.

Ask your child about his/her activities at the beginning of each week. You'd be surprised by what they'll share. This is increasingly important with older children… but, still works with little ones. For instance, my 4-year old reminds me every week that Wednesday is water play day at summer camp!

Do you have an idea of another possible solution? Jot it down, along with an implementation date.

LETTERS TO MY SONS

I'm Sorry

I can't remember a time when either of my parents ever said "I'm sorry" to me as a child.

I don't think it's something that I looked for...but, I definitely remember the first time my mom uttered those words to me as an adult.

To be honest, it made me feel a little weird, because it came completely out of the blue. Plus, it was shortly after she survived her bout with triple negative breast cancer;

a form of cancer with receptor negative – estrogen, progesterone, and HER2 mutations.

While I was on the other end of the phone – I could hear my mom carefully constructing her words as she apologized for anything that she might have done wrong in parenting my two siblings and me. I don't know if it was so unnerving for me because of her former health crisis... or because I just don't like conversations like those. But, it was one of those moments when I decided... if I ever became a parent... I would always say, "Please"... "Thank you", and... "I'm sorry".

~ Love Mom

CHAPTER 5
SACRIFICE V. COMPROMISE

*"She speaks with wisdom,
and faithful instruction is on her tongue."*
~Proverbs 31:26

I have two words that I would like for you to ponder for a moment:

» Sacrifice
» Compromise

When you think of those two words... what comes to mind? The dictionary on my laptop defines *Sacrifice* as:

"An act of giving up something valued for the sake of something else regarded as more important or worthy"

While, Compromise is defined as:

"The acceptance of standards that are lower than is desirable"

I often hear parents use these words when describing how much they sacrifice for their children... or insist that they're uncompromising when it comes to providing the best for their children. But, how many of us actually take the time to explain how... or exactly what we mean?

While I think it's important to shed light on how much we give of ourselves for our child(ren)'s well-being, I find it equally important for our children to understand how they might shape our decisions.

I can remember a childhood friend asking me if I ever felt like my parents were just together because of my siblings and me. I instantly said no... as I, personally, had never felt that way.

But, she quickly clarified her ask, because... based on comments that her mom would make... she often felt like her mom blamed her for needing to remain in a marriage where she wasn't happy. Now, I don't believe her mom ever came out and directly said that, but my friend knew that her mother wasn't happy. Plus, she was constantly told how much her mom sacrificed to give her and her sibling a better life.

I think this weighed heavily on my friend because she started to blame herself for her mom not being happy. Yet, a simple clarification could have remedied the entire situation. Kids have enormous imaginations. We should never leave them guessing about where they stand in our lives.

As a mom who travels quite frequently, I can see how an active child's imagination might have them feeling as though you're traveling so much because you don't want to be home with them. This is why I go above and beyond to ensure that my boys know and understand where Mommy is... and what I'm doing.

For instance, before I travel I talk to them about where I'm going, how long I'll be away, and what I'll be doing while I'm gone. I've noticed that this helps calm them... and makes it clear that I'm not hopping on a plane to get away from them...I'm hopping on a plane to provide for them.

The Battle

Have you ever used the words *sacrifice* or *compromise to* describe how much you give of yourself for your child(ren)?

If so, how can you ensure that all parties understand exactly what you mean when you express how you're giving of yourself?

The Solution

Recognizing that an apology might be the remedy to an existing conflict between you and your child is only half the battle...apologizing is the other.

Be explicitly clear and transparent when sharing information with your children. Don't be afraid to be vulnerable with your kids...you're providing a safety net for them... One that shows them that it's equally ok for them to be transparent with you!

CHAPTER 6

Gettin' Down To Business

*"Her husband has full confidence in her
and lacks nothing of value."*

~Proverbs 31:11

My guess is... if you've made it this far in the book... you understand that there isn't some "magic formula" for managing your life as Mom and Boss. Yet, it's my hope that you've found some applicable nuggets to help your double identities successfully co-exist.

Now, no matter how busy you are... and no matter how much you love your bundles of joy... Mommies have needs too! And if you're anything like me - some nights you might want to cuddle up beside someone warm... who's not your little one!

>> HER THERAPY

So, how can you possibly factor in managing a relationship when you've already got so much on your plate? Well... That's what we're going to tackle in this chapter.

Now, I clearly don't have all the answers, but, I'm willing to share from my experiences and from the experiences of those around me.

As the host of "The Woman Behind The Business®" Talk Show, I've listened to hundreds of women share stories about their entrepreneurial journey. One area that either seems to thrive... or rests dormant... is the vitality of their relationships.

I can totally understand how this can be, as I've personally gone through it.

My story is pretty simple. I was married for about 5-years before I went into business for myself. My husband had a successful career in engineering and I was the journalist-gone-rogue entrepreneur. In the beginning, I didn't know exactly what problem I wanted my business to solve. All I knew was that I would figure it out along the way... and that's pretty much what I did (and continue to do every day).

{68}

I tried to communicate how things were going in business with my spouse (as I know it's extremely important to maintain good communication) but... after coming to feel like money was at the core of what interested him most... my communication eventually ceased.

Of course it was... ultimately...up to me to either sink or swim. But, sadly, I felt like support was lacking.

Now, I can say that he has always made himself available to care for our children, which allowed me to travel and work whatever hours were required. So, I could never bad- mouth my children's father - as I'm sure he was doing the best that he could with a wife who seemed to be more interested in responding to a stranger's email (potential client, in my mind) than a quiet dinner for two. So, there was definitely room for improvement on both sides. I can recall one conversation when he asked if I wanted to just chill out and watch some television... and I responded by telling him that... it wasn't that I didn't want to spend time with him... I was just not interested in wasting time.

I'm not sure if he quite understood what I meant, but... essentially... I was letting him know that if he could figure out

>> HER THERAPY

a way for us to do something together that was also working towards a common goal... I would be all in.

But... at that time in our lives... I felt like I needed to be building my business to provide for my famliy. I didn't feel like I had the luxury of "chilling".

And unfortunately, I know that I'm not the only woman that has felt that way. One young lady on The Woman Behind The Business® Talk Show shared how she felt alone and kind of isolated in her marriage. She was ready to dive into entrepreneurship, yet her husband wasn't interested in supporting her dream. She expressed that, regardless of what she wanted, "he was looking for her financial contribution to the house". So... she left.

On the other end of the spectrum - I've seen husbands and wives weather the storms of their journeys through hell and high water... until they see sunshine and the rainbow on the other side of the struggle.

So, ladies. How do we achieve the latter? How do we turn off our "bossy" nature when we are in the presence of our spouse, man friend, or mere friends? What have other women

{70}

bosses (with children) done to maintain successful romantic relationships?

Well, I've asked some of my most trusted friends, who have been in business from as few as four years to nearly 30 years; and have managed to find love, hold onto it... and overcome "real life" obstacles... to share what they believe were key indicators for their relationship's success.

Who better to start with than my own parents, Tyrone & Veronica Todd. They have been married for 40-years and... for 22 of those years... they've been partners in business. My mom has ventured out and started various businesses over the years - but, their most successful business is the one they built together.

When "Todd's Real Estate Investments & Rentals" was in its infancy, Veronica, had an infant son, and she and her husband both had full-time jobs.

Today, they are parents to three adult children, a handful of grandchildren, and they are functioning in the capacity of small business owners, solely. When asked the secret to their marital and business successes, Veronica quickly attributed those

>> HER THERAPY

successes to both parties maintaining a mutual respect for each other... in and out of the workplace.

"We always maintain a professional demeanor in front of others," says Veronica. "When we're in the workplace, I address him as "Mr. Todd," not as my husband. That's out of respect for our professional relationship and our team members. "

"At the end of the day I'm a team player and- as the head of the company - I know my team looks up to me." Imagine one day I walk into the office calling my husband, "Honey" and "Sweetie". Then... the next day... he's pissed me off and I'm calling him by his first name... that's too open.

I don't like for people to be able to read whatever might be going on in our relationship, so, when we're in the workplace, we maintain a mutual level of respect... for each other and our craft. Therefore, no one ever really knows who we are to one another, unless we decide to tell them."

Ms. Karla has been married for 38-years and recently celebrated her 28th year in business! As the mother of four... one of whom has special needs... she found herself struggling to feel fulfilled during her 40's.

"I was a mess in my 40's," Karla explained. "I was in the house every day caring for my child, and running an in-home childcare facility. Then... there came a time in my life where I just wanted more. I didn't feel like my husband was doing enough to show me love, yet all the while he would buy me surprise gifts year round... and yet it wasn't enough.

So... I cheated.

I thought I 'deserved' more. I thought I was supposed to have a lavish house, fancy clothing... you know... all of the material things. I didn't realize that I had so much more than all of those things combined in the little house that God gave me... because it was filled with love.

>> HER THERAPY

In my situation, my husband wasn't the problem. He was the solution. He prayed for me, even when I was doing wrong. He stood by my side. So, when you ask me what has been the secret to our success... I'd have to say having a praying husband."

Tressa "Azarel" Smallwood, an award-winning book publisher and the mastermind behind MegaMind Media, has been married for 23 of the 18-years that her firm has been in existence. Prior to launching her American Film and Production Company (that specializes in book-to-film adaptations and original television series and programming), Tressa was a school teacher.

So, how did she successfully transition from a 9-5 to full blown entrepreneur... and sustain her marriage? Well, she had a slight advantage because her husband is also an entrepreneur. I say that it's a benefit because her husband understands what it takes to create a vision, develop it out, and execute it. He won't get mad if she isn't able to call him throughout the day or escape for an unscheduled lunch.

Now that latter statement is what leads us to what Tressa says is the winning ingredient to their union - "We are very intentional with how our time is spent. It is literally a challenge

>> HER THERAPY

because we have to schedule everything. For instance, certain nights, we have cell phone restrictions. Other times we request an entire block of time. But, mutually, we have decided that spending quality time with one another is important. And while being "penciled in" might not sound sexy... it's the launching pad for us to stay connected."

LaToya White is the Founder and CEO of Sylver Rain Consulting, an IT firm based in Washington, DC. She's a 39-year old mother of two boys and has been married for 11-years. In the latter four years of her marriage, she took on a new challenge and... with the support of her husband... she decided it was time to add small business owner to her list of titles.

"I probably would have never launched Sylver Rain if my husband hadn't shown his unwavering faith and trust in my ability to build a successful business," says LaToya. "I can recall one of our conversations, during the time that I was straddling the fence on leaving my full-time job and starting a business - and he said something that I'll never forget. He said, 'I will take on a second job, if necessary, just so you can rest assured that all of the bills will be paid.' That sealed the deal for me. I knew that, if I had his full support, I could do the rest.

>> HER THERAPY

Since then, he continues to support me by allowing me to travel as necessary for business trips, and if I need him to grab the boys in the evening or drop them off for school... he handles that too."

When you have a partner who is supportive of your vision... it's a beautiful thing. While he might not be intricately involved in the business... he trusts me. He has faith in me... and for that I am eternally grateful and appreciative of him."

Take a moment to jot down these 4 key support questions provided by my Mom/Boss friends:

- » Does Mutual Respect exist?
- » Is he willing to pray for you?
- » Does he Schedule Quality Time?
- » Does he trust in your abilities and have enough faith to support your dreams?

The married perspective can sometimes feel far-fetched when you've been lied to, cheated on, and neglected. So, I asked one of my friends who has endured some of those aforementioned obstacles to share her perspective on finding love as a single Mom/Boss.

{78}

Today, she embraces the possibility of entering into a relationship... and has opened up about her experiences to offer us an unflinching look at some of the reasons why marriages fail.

To begin, allow me to introduce you to my girl Tara Gates Anderson, CEO of TGA Unified, LLC, a branding and media company designed to create, develop, and expand brands, including those of professional athletes. Well, about 10 years before she launched her business, Tara endured a pretty devastating personal situation.

Her husband of less than 12-months committed adultery... and the outcome of his actions was an innocent baby boy by his mistress. At the time, Tara had recently given birth to their beautiful daughter, Ava.

This situation would have shattered a lot of us. But, not Tara. It actually propelled her. Instead of allowing that circumstance to define the rest of her life... she leaned on family and friends to help her through to the next phase... which included the birth of TGA Unified, LLC.

Over the past 20-years Tara has been in long-term relationships, while also embracing her time alone.

>> HER THERAPY

"I don't have to settle", says Tara. "I recognize that I have a strong personality... meaning I come with a different type of "armor". I've been a single parent and a business owner- so, a man needs to 'come correct' when he comes for me. I won't settle for a man not being accountable. I won't settle for a man who is not honest. Nor will I hold my breath, hoping that a man will change into someone else. I have had conversations with my guy friends about this very conversation and they all agree that... whoever 'my guy' is... he has to be ready for me as a woman and as a person.

And... for myself... I'm finally at a place where I'm 'open'. I am comfortable with where I am in business. I'm happy with myself as a woman, a person, and a human being. Therefore, I am not only ready to give love - I am also ready to receive it.

One element that I've enjoyed from past relationships is mutual leading. While I know I was being led by him - he was open to me leading him as well. I absolutely loved that reciprocity of growth. When a man can support you and believe in you... and you can reciprocate... it's amazing.

My dad always told me that you know when you've found love because it's easy. If you aren't experiencing that and it's hard... then love's not there.

{80}

Then, there's me. I'm an all or nothing type of individual. I drown when I attempt to tread in unfamiliar emotional waters, not because I'm not willing to try. But, because I know who I am…and most importantly what I need to thrive.

I got divorced 6-months shy of our 10-year wedding anniversary. In our circumstance we didn't dissolve our relationship (as he would call it) because of violence, adultery, or probably any of the typical reasons that's deemed appropriate by societal standards. But, I felt like I wasn't being supported and he felt like I wasn't spending enough time with him. Now, if I were to be completely transparent with where I felt the problems began…I'd have to say that it aligned with when I transitioned into full-time business ownership.

I can recall telling him that I'm a different B.E.A.S.T. when it comes to building a business. When I'm in building mode my work ethic goes into overdrive and I'm willing to make sacrifices to get the business positioned for revenue generation and sustainability. So, my focus changed. But, not without warning. In business I believe that you must have a strong village. Your village is made up of your essential support team. If your spouse is part of your village they have to offer you something that is unique and special to their position in your life. If your spouse doesn't have the capacity to provide the emotional support you need - you have to determine the best way to keep them engaged with your business...even if they're not a part of your village. This is where I was unsuccessful. I lacked the desire to include my ex-husband in any part of my business because I felt as though he was only interested in the company's financials.

Of course there were other issues that eventually led to the demise of the marriage - however, this is the role I played. Since I am an all or nothing type person, I desire to share all aspects of who I am with my partner.

When I start compartmentalizing what I can share with my partner...that's when the guards surface and the lack of transparency emerges.

So, evaluate what's important to you and what, if anything, you'll require from your partner as a business owner.

The Battle

When it comes to support, do you feel as though you're receiving the type of support you'd like?

What would you say is the number-one pitfall that you run into during relationships?

Review your answers and attempt to apply the Q.U.I.E.T method from the previous chapter. While it was designed for your relationship with your children - it can be applied to any relationship.

What areas might you be able to improve upon when it comes to maintaining your relationship.

Is there a secret ingredient to your relationship that you would like to share? We'd like to know - please share it at www.hertherapy.net

The Solution

Based on the responses from those in successful relationships, you should keep the following in consideration:

- » Mutual Respect
- » Prayer - *Will he pray for you?*
- » Schedule Quality Time
- » Faith & Trust - *Does he trust in your abilities to succeed and does he have enough faith to support your dreams?*

Chapter 7
The Proverbs Woman

*"A wife of noble character who can find?
She is worth far more than rubies."*

~Proverbs 31:10

One evening I was washing dishes after the boys and I had dinner... and various character traits of what I deemed to make up a "good woman," started running through my mind. I embraced my randomness, and shortly thereafter, I thought about my line sister, Ashley, who had once suggested that I incorporate the Proverbs Woman into one of my business ideas.

>> HER THERAPY

In that moment I realized that I wasn't merely having another random thought... I was actually being instructed that this was that time.

If you flip back through the quotes that led into every chapter of this book, you'll notice that each one is a different verse from Proverbs 31.

While I think most people equate Proverbs 31 to showcasing the characteristics of a "good wife" - I think it shows a noble woman at various stages in her life.

Now, I'm no pastor and I'm the furthest thing from perfect, but, for me... when I read about the Proverbs Woman... it reminds me of the "many" women I strive to be on any given day... most often, all in the same day.

Since this book is about harnessing the powers that exists in being Mom and Boss, I found it ever so interesting... when I went back to read the entire chapter of Proverbs 31... to find that the first 9 verses are between a mother and her son, who happens to be King.

She is counseling him on what it means to be a noble man. While she recognizes him as the King - she still warns him against potential harms that can invade his life: drinking, choosing unworthy women and being unjust.

It's not until she lays the foundation of what he needs to be that the chapter moves on to what a noble woman should be.

As the mother of two boys, I can see myself having a very similar conversation with my Kings. I want them to chose a virtuous woman, just like the mother speaking to her son in Proverbs 31. It's my interpretation that the passages that follow, in the book of Proverbs, are attributes that the mother wants her son to equate to outstanding Godly Woman traits

Personally, they're all traits that I would desire for both of my sons to find in a woman. Even more importantly... it's my prayer that they grow up seeing these qualities in me.

To take it one step further... if these are characteristics that we all desire for our young Kings to eventually find in their Queen... it's only logically that... somewhere... there is a King who's looking for you... a wife of noble character!

LETTERS TO MY SONS

Vision 2020: The Reset

When mommy first started writing this book in 2019, our lives looked a lot different. However, a shift occurred almost immediately after the "much anticipated" new year began.

Personally, our family experienced a number of massive transitions:

- » Our once single family home was split into two

- » COVID-19 pulled you away from your teachers and friends

>> HER THERAPY

» We moved the same day the schools closed

» Mommy and daddy divorced

» Your home-school teacher (mommy) isn't as patient as your original kindergarten and first grade teachers

» You went an entire month only seeing your dad through a screen

...and I'm sure I could keep adding things to the list if time permitted.

The point I'm attempting to make is that – I want to recognize the two of you for being troopers through it all. You have maintained your honor roll status at school. And even in moments of feeling consumed with emotions and fighting to find the best way to channel your worked up energy – I am proud of you for showing up every day with an open mind, heart and spirit.

What you are enduring, mommy doesn't make light of it. To be honest, I can't recall ever going through any of these monumental changes as a child. That's why this final letter in this book is to let you know that I celebrate you.

As life throws us her best shot, we continue to respond with grace, peace and hope. It's not easy, however it is very admirable to watch you two navigate through these times with assurance and comfort.

It's my prayer that you feel supported, valuable and loved.

I recognize that mommy is far from perfect...however, I believe that I was hand selected to raise you, groom you, and teach you the ways of the world.

I am honored to hold the title as "Mom". However, I am most proud to watch you grow into faithful men of God.

>> HER THERAPY

Continue to walk in the path that God has ordained over your lives. As you do, you'll come to see that blessings will flow from the crowns of your heads to the soles of your feet. Believe me...I'm a living witness.

~ Love Mom

Resources

> *"Listen to advice and accept instruction,
> that you may gain wisdom in the future."*
> ~Proverbs 19:20

ABC's of Balancing Motherhood & Business

AFFIRMATIONS
Start your day with good intentions, speaking positivity over the day ahead.

BOUNDARIES
Create clear boundaries for your employer (clients) and your family.

CELEBRATE
Take a moment to celebrate each of your wins... no matter how small. This is especially important on hard days!

>> HER THERAPY

D ELEGATE
Don't try to do it all by yourself. While you might not have a team of people at your disposal - think of ways you can spend your time smartly (i.e instead of going into the grocery store - hire someone to deliver your groceries to your door).

E XERCISE
You and the kids will appreciate a little workout in between all the hard work you'll be tackling.

F UN
Have fun. Don't get so wrapped up in all the work you have to complete. Remember you can have fun while getting things done.

G OALS
Set realistic goals for yourself, especially when you are managing multiple roles.

H APPINESS
Take full responsibility for your happiness. Don't allow others to influence or place limitations on what's important to you.

INVEST

Invest in some projects or programs that you've been wanting to accomplish. There's no better time than now to start working towards your personal goals.

JUSTIFY

If you are participating in an online meeting or conference call and you have young children who might cause noise or interruptions... be sure to let the facilitator know before an incident occurs. It is also wise to exercise the use of your mute button.

KEEPSAKE

Create a keepsake journal of your time at home with your family / kids. Think about it. When was the last time that you really had quality time with them. Don't be afraid to share your work with your kids. You just might be surprised by their level of interest.

LIST

Create lists to help you better track items you need to manage, purchase, execute.

>> HER THERAPY

MEDITATION
Close each day out with a meditation. Think of all of the things you were able to accomplish throughout the course of the day. Now show yourself and the universe gratitude for your successes.

NO
Don't be afraid to tell people NO. You know your limitations and you shouldn't feel guilty for protecting your well-being.

OBLIGATE
Don't over obligate yourself. Take a hard look at what you can realistically manage and stay within your means.

PREPARE
If you know you have a busy work schedule plan the children's activities accordingly (i.e. conference call - schedule the kids to watch a movie during that time - but, have popcorn and other snacks prepared ahead of time)

QUIET TIME
Allocate some time just for you. Whether this is during

{96}

the kids recess or once they go to bed...set aside your "me time"
to refresh and refuel.

R EVIEW
Review activities and commitments for the coming week
so you can prepare accordingly.

S CHEDULE
Literally outline (hour by hour) the activities for the day.
Children are used to routines - while they might not be in
school - they still need to know what the plan is for the day. You
can start with the basics - reading block, snack, lunch, recess...
and fill in the remainder of the day with school work.

T ASKS
Execute your most important tasks first thing in the
morning.

U NWIND
This is the perfect time to prove to yourself that you can
unwind and still be productive. Give yourself the freedom to
explore new things while staying on top of your responsibilities.

>> HER THERAPY

VOICE
If you're experiencing anxiety over any area of your life - don't be afraid to vocalize it. Your voice matters and deserves to be heard.

WATER
Drink lots of water. Hydration helps with productivity.

XRAY
Examine areas that you can improve upon daily. Don't beat yourself up...we can all do some things better. The goal is to take steps to get better...even if they're baby steps.

YES
Give yourself permission to do something special for yourself. Trust me...you deserve it. Say Yes!

ZEN
Enjoy daily moments of peace and relaxation.

Thank You

> *"Behold, children are a heritage from the LORD,*
> *The fruit of the womb a reward."*
> ~Psalm 127:3

This book is written for every mother who struggles to comfort the complexities that are her babies. When you go through the birthing process of a physical being or a vision...your worlds immediately co-exist. It's never really a question of what's most important to you, while at times things can appear foggy.

I pray that this book serves as a reminder that there is no right or wrong way to raise *your* child. God entrusted them to you specifically, because you hold the keys to raising them to be dynamic men or powerful women. Even if you gave life to your babies through adoption or as a foster parent...you were chosen before the child was ever conceived to step into the role that God required for their life.

Thank you for joining me on this journey...I pray that you enjoyed the insights...but, I'm most excited to learn how you'll implement new traditions, the Q.U.I.E.T. Method, and any other tool that you've gained from this book. So, now that I've done my part in writing **Her Therapy**, can you share your thoughts about the book on our Amazon page?

Just because you've made it to the end of the book, doesn't mean that this is where the story ends. I'd like for us to stay connected. Please be sure to follow @angelnlivas on your favorite social media platforms, and subscribe to the "Woman Behind The Business" Talk Show on your preferred podcast platform.

Lastly, you can join our therapeutic online community at hertherapy.net

This is only the beginning...

About The Author

"Do you not believe that I am in the Father and the Father is in me? The words that I say to you I do not speak on my own authority, but the Father who dwells in me does his works."
~John 14:10

Angel N. Livas is a best-selling author, visionary, CEO, and 2019 Communicator award recipient for her radio program, "The Woman Behind The Business Talk Show."

In 2016, Angel organized a movement for women entrepreneurs to expand their companies into international territories by way of her non-profit, "The Woman Behind

The Business." Since its inception, women from across the globe annually convene in Nassau, Bahamas, where the first international chapter was formed.

As the CEO of DC Media Connection, Angel utilizes her keen sense of video production and content creation to attract her clients to their ideal consumers. Recently, Angel was named "Woman to Watch 2020 for Business Excellence" by the Creative Life Institute. In 2016, Angel was highlighted in the Washington Business Journal under "People On The Move" and named "Influential Business Woman of 2016" by AI Magazine.

Before embarking upon her entrepreneurial journey, Angel oversaw six-nationally syndicated talk-radio shows, which included producing programming for award-winning celebrity hosts Larry King and Jane Pauley.

Today, she uses storytelling as a tool to connect to the hearts of audiences as she graces global stages from Accra, Ghana, to moderating conversations throughout the Caribbean. Angel is a proud lady of Alpha Kappa Alpha Sorority, Incorporated, and a graduate of Howard University, where she graduated magna cum laude. She received her Master of Arts from the American University and she is also the recipient of two professional certifications from Stanford University and Rutgers University. Angel currently resides in Northern Virginia with her two children.

LET'S STAY CONNECTED

Join our network:
www.hertherapy.net

Follow the author on:
Instagram - Facebook - LinkedIn - Twitter
@angelnlivas

Find out about other works and
upcoming author events:
www.angelnlivas.com

CPSIA information can be obtained
at www.ICGtesting.com
Printed in the USA
LVHW090501110520
655341LV00003B/989